The New York Dog Owner's Guide

Everything You and Your Dog Need
to Know About Life in the City

The New York Dog Owner's Guide

Everything You and Your Dog Need to Know About Life in the City

Martha Kaplan

With Illustrations by Charles Barsotti

CITY & COMPANY
NEW YORK

City & Company
175 Fifth Avenue, Suite 2255
New York, NY 10010

Printed in the United States of America

Design by Stacie Chaiken

Library of Congress Cataloguing-in-Publication Data:
Kaplan, Martha
The New York dog owner's guide: everything you and
your dog need to know about life in the City / by
Martha Kaplan; illustrations by Charles Barsotti.
p. cm.
ISBN 1-885492-02-2: $9.95
1. Dogs—New York (N.Y.) I. Title.
SF427.K325 1994
636.7'0887'097471—dc20   94 - 26455
                                            CIP

First printing October 1994
10 9 8 7 6 5 4 3 2 1

Acknowledgments

I'd like to thank every dog lover who shared dog stories and dog information with me, but especially Dale Demy, Pat McGregor, Robin Kovary, Bern Marcowitz, and Margot Rosenberg.

Thanks also to Jane Magidson and the crew at City & Company: Kristin Frederickson, Stacie Chaiken, Lois Wyse and, of course, Helene Silver. And most of all to Charles Barsotti for his wonderful illustrations.

🐾 M.K. 🐾

Table of Contents

Introduction

Owning a dog in New York can be a wonderful experience or it can be a headache. The difference between the two is knowledge.

This little guide gives both new and experienced dog owners a look at the range of services, supplies, and resources available. This information should make life easier and more enjoyable for both you and your dog.

New York is a unique city that offers unique opportunities for dog owners. Here you can find singing dog groomers, dog psychics, acupuncturists, masseuses, homeopathic vets, even an artist to immortalize Rover on a hand-hooked rug. You can have a bark mitzvah or bring pooch to church for a blessing.

We've made no attempt to list all of the resources available in the city—for that just flip through the *Yellow Pages*. Nor are we endorsing any of those we include and suggest that you verify the reliability of any service you use. Prices are obviously subject to change.

We now invite you to turn the page and explore with us everything you need to know about what this one-of-a-kind city holds for you and your best friend.

Be Prepared

So you think you want to get a dog.

Maybe you have fond memories of the dog you had as a child. Maybe you loved Lassie, Lady and the Tramp, Asta, or Rin Tin Tin. Maybe you should think again.

Owning a dog in New York City is a big commitment. If you live in the country or the suburbs, when Norton has to go out early in the morning, all you have to do is open the back door. In the city, it's not so simple. First you have to get dressed. Then you have to put on the leash, get a baggie or some newspapers for pooper-scooping, and lock up the apartment. You stay out until the dog has done its business. All this not just once, but two or three times a day.

Owning a dog is a major responsibility. Consider the following before getting a dog:

1. You must get up and go out for a walk every morning with the dog—rain, snow, sleet, or hail, and no matter how sick or tired you feel.

2. Home right after work. A movie or a party is fine, but first home to feed and walk the pooch.

3. You love those special imported Italian shoes, but you forgot to put them out of puppy's reach. Rush home immediately.

4. You would love to have a navy blue sofa but the dog has tan hair and sheds.

5. Sure, let's go away for the weekend. Oops, they don't like dogs.

6. You hate the thought of pooper-scooping.

7. You can't stand dog hairs on your clothing.

8. You think getting the dog trained is a waste of time.

9. You want wall-to-wall white carpet.

10. You're allergic.

If any of these statements make you think twice about getting a dog, do yourself and the dog a favor: don't. But if you are willing to take on the responsibility and realize that your time will no longer be all your own, the experience can be rewarding and fulfilling.

Getting the Dog

So now you know the pitfalls. If, however, you are still determined to get a dog, the next decision is what kind of dog to get. Many people are happy with lovable mutts; others want full pedigrees. If you don't know what type of dog you want, your neighborhood dog run or park is a good place to do some research. Dog owners are incredibly friendly and forthcoming when asked to talk about their pets. They will tell you how wonderful their particular dog is (don't count on objectivity here), where they got it, and what type of care it needs. Certain breeds require a lot of exercise. If you're not interested in taking a long walk every day, don't get a terrier. If you don't see yourself wielding a brush on a regular basis, don't get a long-haired collie.

After you've looked around the dog run, go to dog shows, talk to trainers and dog walkers, or visit the local bookstore for one of the many books on different breeds. *The Roger Carras Dog Book* (M. Evans and Company) describes most breeds, rates them for apartment living and tells you how much care and grooming each breed needs. Check a breed before you buy. An otter hound may look adorable as a puppy, but it weighs more than one hundred pounds at maturity, and it just may decide to hunt down the sweet little kitten that hangs out at the local vegetable stand if no otters are around.

If your heart is set on a purebred, visit several breeders. Otherwise, consider an adoption agency. You can also go to your local pet supply shop or veterinarian. They often post signs and pictures of dogs of all ages, sizes, and breeds that are looking for a home.

Dogs Sources in the New York City Area:

ASPCA ADOPTION CENTERS

Bronx:
1 Fordham Plaza
718-733-0744

Brooklyn:
2336 Linden Boulevard
718-272-7200

Manhattan:
424 East 92nd Street
326 East 110th Street
212-876-7700

Queens:
92-29 Queens Boulevard
Rego Park
718-997-6331

Staten Island:
1490 Richmond Avenue
718-370-0679

Rescued puppies, mutts, and even a few pedigreed dogs are available here for adoption. A $55 donation covers adoption, a medical examination, initial shots (including rabies), free spaying or neutering, and a travel kit so you can take the dog home. You'll need two pieces of identification (one with an address), and before you can leave with any animal, the organization speaks with every adult member of your family and checks references.

BIDE-A-WEE
410 East 38th Street, Manhattan
212-532-4455

Last year, this organization placed close to fourteen
hundred dogs of all sorts and varieties in New York
City. If you are looking for a particular breed, let them
know and they will contact you when one is available.
A $55 donation covers medical exam, initial shots, neu-
tering or spaying. If the dog is over six months old, it
has already been spayed or neutered, so the requested
donation is $30. Expect to provide proof of identifica-
tion and references (including landlord); there is also
an interview.

HUMANE SOCIETY OF NEW YORK
306 East 59th Street, Manhattan
212-752-4840

Dogs of all sorts and ages of are available for adoption
here. The application form requests your employer's
name, two references, and identification with address.
They ask for a donation of $50. Spaying or neutering
an adopted puppy costs $25 ($10 off their regular
price). An older dog will already be fixed.

PROSPECT PARK DOG OUTREACH GROUP
Brooklyn
718-832-2724

This group helps find homes for dogs rescued throughout Brooklyn—all breeds or no breeds—any size or age.
Call to find out what's available. They are also looking
for foster homes where the dogs can stay until they are
adopted. Donations are welcome.

NORTH SHORE ANIMAL LEAGUE

25 Davis Avenue
Port Washington, Long Island
516-883-7575

A constantly changing and very large selection of older dogs and puppies is usually available. You can fill out a request form for special breeds. As with several other shelters, North Shore says it never destroys a dog. The suggested $50 donation covers a medical examination, shots, neutering or spaying, a travel kit so you can get the dog home safely, and veterinary care for thirty days. They do a thorough interview, ask for (and check) references, and may visit your home after the adoption to make sure the dog is in good hands. We have seen them turn away a family that wanted to adopt a puppy, but showed little interest in treating the animal properly.

BEING KIND

212-781-4888

This organization rescues abandoned dogs of all types and ages and tries to find them proper homes. Call for availability.

AMERICAN KENNEL CLUB

900-407-PUPS

Although not a direct source for dogs itself, the club can point you in the right direction if you are looking for a specific breed. They can give you the name of a breeder representative who works with dog clubs and breeders near you.

RETIRED GREYHOUNDS AS PETS (REGAP)
P.O. Box 76
Bethany, CT 06525
203-467-7407

Once greyhound race dogs are finished at the track, they are usually destroyed. Very gentle and quite beautiful, these dogs have had a horrendous sporting life; for example, some have had all their teeth pulled. It's a worthwhile rescue if you're interested.

GREYHOUND PETS OF AMERICA
800-366-1472

Your call will be forwarded to the nearest chapter.

Veterinarians and Alternative Care

Picking a veterinarian is one of the most important decisions you will be making for you and your dog. Ask friends and neighbors for referrals. Speak to someone at your local pet supply shop or your trainer or dog walker. And since there are many breed-specific conditions, find out how much experience the vet has had with your particular breed.

Make yourselves comfortable.

If you're the kind of person who asks a lot of questions, be sure to choose a vet who is willing to take the time to answer them. And although Rover can't put his opinion of the vet into words, his behavior will tell you a lot. Just as there is no reason for a child to be afraid of the pediatrician, there is no reason your dog should be terrified of the vet. Watch how the vet behaves with your dog. If he or she does not take time to comfort a frightened animal, this probably isn't the vet for you.

Location.

You want to be able to get to the vet quickly and easily. Since very few New Yorkers can hop into a car and drive to the vet, the closer the better. Also keep the size of your dog in mind. It is no problem to tote a sick Westie, but if your Lab has to be carried to the vet, you want one nearby. Don't count on being able to hail a cab either. Drivers are not eager to pick up a passenger with a sick dog.

Referrals.

More than two hundred vets are registered with the Veterinary Medical Association of New York City. For referrals, call them at 212-246-0057.

Emergency hours.

Make sure your veterinarian either has them or can refer you to someone who does. In case of emergency, call your own vet first. If he or she is not available, you can go to the Animal Medical Center at 510 East 62nd Street in Manhattan (212-838-8100). This is the only place in the city that is fully staffed twenty-four hours a day and it has excellent emergency facilities.

A sampling of facilities that have extended hours or services follows:

Manhattan

ASPCA, BERGH MEMORIAL HOSPITAL
424 East 92nd Street
212-876-7700
Hours—Mon-Fri: 9 A.M. to 7 P.M.; Sat: 9 A.M. to 3 P.M.

ANIMAL EMERGENCY CLINIC
240 East 80th Street
212-988-1000
Hours—9 A.M. to 1 A.M.; 365 days a year.

ANIMAL MEDICAL CENTER
510 East 62 Street
212-838-8100
Hours—24 hours a day; 365 days a year.

BIDE-A-WEE
410 East 38th Street
212-532-5884
Hours—Mon-Fri: 9:30 A.M. to 3 P.M.; Thurs: 9:30 A.M.
to 3 P.M. and 5 P.M. to 7 P.M.; Sat: 9 A.M. to 1:30 P.M.

CENTER FOR VETERINARY CARE
236 East 75th Street
212-734-7480
Hours—by appointment, Mon and Fri: 9 A.M. to 5:30
P.M.; Tues, Wed, and Thurs: 9 A.M. to 7:30 P.M.; Sat:
9 A.M. to 2:30 P.M.; 24-hour emergency service.

COLUMBIA ANIMAL HOSPITAL
229 West 101st Street
212-864-1144
Hours—Mon-Sat: 9 A.M. to 5 P.M.; 24-hour emergency
service.

EAST BAY ANIMAL CLINIC
612 Second Avenue
212-481-7999
Hours—Mon, Wed, and Fri: 9 A.M. to 12 P.M. and
4 P.M. to 6 P.M.; Tues and Thurs: 4 P.M. to 8 P.M.; Sat:

9 A.M. to 1 P.M.; Sun: 10 A.M. to 3 P.M.; 24-hour emergency service.

LEXINGTON VETERINARY GROUP
133 East 39th Street
212-889-7778
Hours—Mon-Wed: 9 A.M. to 5:30 P.M.; Thurs: 9 A.M. to 7:30 P.M.; Fri and Sat: 9 A.M. to 12:30 P.M.; 24-hour emergency service.

MANHATTAN VETERINARY GROUP
240 East 80th Street
212-988-1000
Hours—by appointment, Mon-Sat: 8 A.M. to 5 P.M. Emergencies, Mon-Sat: 6 P.M. to 1 A.M.; Sun: 11 A.M. to 12 A.M.

PARK EAST ANIMAL HOSPITAL
52 East 64th Street
212-832-8417
Hours—Mon and Thurs: 9 A.M. to 6:30 P.M.; Tues, Wed, and Fri: 9 A.M. to 4:30 P.M.; Sat: 10 A.M. to 3:30 P.M.; Sun: 10:30 A.M. to 3 P.M.; 24-hour emergency service.

UNIVERSITY ANIMAL HOSPITAL
354 East 66th Street
212-288-8884
Hours—Mon-Fri: 8 A.M. to 8 P.M.; Sat: 9 A.M. to 4 P.M.; Sun: 9 A.M. to 1 P.M.; 24-hour emergency service.

WESTSIDE VETERINARY CENTER

220 West 83rd Street
212-580-1800
Hours—Mon to Thurs: 10 A.M. to 9 P.M.; Fri to Sun:
10 A.M. to 5:30 P.M.; 24-hour emergency service.

Outside Manhattan

AAAA ANIMAL MEDICINE AND SURGERY CLINIC

9518 Avenue L
Brooklyn
718-444-5151
Hours—Mon-Fri: 9:30 A.M. to 7:30 P.M.; Sat: 10 A.M.
to 5 P.M.; Sun: 10 A.M. to 3 P.M. Emergencies, seven
days a week: 8 P.M. to midnight. Ambulette service
available.

BROOKLYN VETERINARY EMERGENCY SERVICE

453 Bay Ridge Avenue
Brooklyn
718-748-5180
Hours—Mon-Fri: 8 P.M. to 9 A.M.; Sat: 4 P.M. to 9 A.M.;
Sun: 2 P.M. to 9 A.M. Open 24 hours on holidays.

VETERINARY CENTER

1293 Clove Road
Staten Island
718-720-4211
Hours—by appointment, Mon-Fri: 8 A.M. to 2 P.M.; no
appointment necessary, 8 P.M. to 8 A.M. and on
weekends.

House Calls

The following places make house calls:

Manhattan

A HOUSE CALL SERVICE
349 East 49th Street
212-838-2560

A HOUSE CALL FOR PETS
240 West 10th Street
212-989-2569

AMY I. ATTAS, D.V.M.
101 West 57th Street
212-581-PETS

EAST MANHATTAN ANIMAL CLINIC
1598 Third Avenue
212-722-0528

HOME VETERINARY SERVICES
340 East 80th Street
212-421-0553

PARK EAST ANIMAL HOSPITAL
52 East 64th Street
212-832-8417

ST. MARK'S VETERINARY HOSPITAL
348 East 9th Street
212-477-2688

Outside Manhattan

ALL PETS ANIMAL HOSPITAL

277 Van Duzer Street
Staten Island
718-442-1117

MOBILE VETERINARY UNIT

94 Avenue U
Brooklyn
718-373-0240

PARK SLOPE ANIMAL KIND VETERINARY HOSPITAL

408 Seventh Avenue
Brooklyn
718-832-3899

PET HAVEN ANIMAL HOSPITAL

290 McDonald Avenue
Brooklyn
718-435-6900

SALEM SMALL ANIMAL HOSPITAL

1409 Richmond Avenue
Staten Island
718-370-0700

Alternative Medicine

The many heathcare choices require that you become a knowledgeable consumer. People take their dogs to acupuncturists, chiropractors, and herbalists for anything from pain relief to preventive medicine, or just on a whim. The choice is yours, so keep your pet's well-being in mind.

A good referral source for doctors with a naturalistic approach is the animal health food store, Whiskers, at 235 East 9th Street in Manhattan; the phone number is 1-800-WHISKERS. They have a health club, publish a bimonthly newsletter, and hold regular seminars on holistic animal care. Other referral sources are the American Holistic Veterinary Medical Association, 2214 Old Emerson Road, Bel Air, MD 21015, telephone: 410-569-0795; and the International Veterinary Acupuncture Society, 2140 Conestoga Road, Chester Springs, PA 19425; telephone: 215-827-7245.

Following is a list of a few New York-area vets specializing in alternative medicine:

CENTER FOR VETERINARY CARE
236 East 75th Street
Manhattan
212-734-7480

EAST VILLAGE VETERINARIAN
241 Eldridge Street
Manhattan
212-674-8640

MARTIN GOLDSTEIN ASSOCIATES
400 Smithridge Road
South Salem, NY
914-533-6066

SUE ANN LESSER
20 Burgess Avenue
South Huntington, NY
516-423-9223

ALAN SCHOEN
Brookfarm Veterinary Clinic
Patterson, NY
914-878-4833

Natural Products—Mail Order

L AND H VITAMINS
37-10 Crescent Street
Long Island City, NY 11101
800-221-1152

Natural vitamins, supplements, herbs, and
homeopathic remedies

NATURAL PET CARE COMPANY
8050 Lake City Way NE
Seattle, WA 98115
800-962-8266

Health-care products and vitamins

LOVING TOUCH ANIMAL CENTER
5398 East Mountain Street
Stone Mountain, GA 30083
404-498-5956

Homeopathic animal first-aid kit

Reading

Brennan, Mary L., and Norma Eckroate, *The Natural
Dog* (Plume Publishers)

Macleod, G., *Dogs: Homeopathic Remedies*
(C.W. Daniel Company, Ltd.)

Pitcaim, Richard, *Natural Health for Dogs*
(Rodale Press)

Laws and Etiquette

Laws

An unruly dog not only makes life miserable, its behavior may be against the law. Here are the most important New York dog laws:

All dogs are required to have a license.
To get a license, call the Dog License Program at the Department of Health (212-566-2456). A license costs $8.50 a year ($10.50 for late

renewals). The back of each license reads, "If I'm lost, please call 212-876-7700;" the front displays your dog's license number. Keep a copy of this number at home.

All dogs must be vaccinated for rabies.
Since rabies has reached epidemic levels in the New York City area, this is more than law; it's good sense. You'd be cruel to let your dog go about unvaccinated.

You must pick up after your dog.
Here's the 1-2-3 of pooper-scooping: 1) tuck a small plastic bag in your pocket whenever you go out with your dog; 2) use it as a glove when picking up the offending poop; 3) drop the bag in the nearest trash can. Fastidious types may prefer a white or opaque bag.

When walking Rover, you must keep him on a leash no more than six feet long.
Again, good sense and the law go hand in hand. The leash keeps your dog from running away, jumping up on people, scaring little kids, knocking down old folks, and running off into traffic.

If your dog is a guard dog or trained to attack, it must wear a tag identifying it as such.

You must also post an identifying sign at your front door.

The Department of Health has the right to examine any animal that is the subject of a bite report or complaint.
If the animal is found to be vicious or dangerous, you may be ordered to have it muzzled, permanently removed from the city, or taken for "the purpose of humane destruction." If your dog shows the slightest tendency to bite, go to a good trainer immediately or keep it muzzled around other people and dogs.

Dog Etiquette

DO teach your dog not to bark when left alone if you live in an apartment. Dogs can be trained not to bark incessantly, and not to cry and howl when you leave. You will be doing yourself, your neighbors, and your dog a favor.

DO ask the owner of another dog approaching on the street if the dog is friendly. Breaking up a dog fight can be horrendous and dangerous. By the same token, do keep your dog away from other dogs if you know that he or she is aggressive and likely to attack.

DO learn the "leash ballet" maneuver. When two dog owners with leashed dogs meet, the dogs circle each other and sniff. To keep the leashes from becoming entangled, the owners must turn and circle. After one or two such meetings, you'll become adept at the dance. This is a training process for the owners, not the dogs.

DO be prepared to give up your own identity when you're walking a dog. Once you're attached to a leash, you only exchange dog names. People who see the same people and dogs on daily walks over the years know the dogs' names, but not the owners'. It's always "Peaches' father" or "Harry's mom."

DO keep your dog away from anyone who is afraid of dogs. You may know that your dog is sweet and loving and only wants to jump up and say hello, but all a total stranger sees is a dog lunging at him.

The American Kennel Club has a good citizen award for dogs. Even if your dog does not participate in the program (see below) you should teach it to:

1. Accept a friendly stranger quietly

2. Sit politely for petting

3. Welcome grooming and examination by someone it doesn't know

4. Walk on a loose leash without pulling or straining when you walk, turn, or stop

5. Walk through a crowd

6. Sit and lie down on command, and stay in place

7. Calm down quickly and easily after play or lots of praise

8. Behave politely around other dogs

9. Remain calm around distractions

10. Remain calm when left alone

For more information about this program, contact the American Kennel Club, Attention: CGC, 5580 Centerview Drive, Suite 200, Raleigh, NC 27606; telephone: 919-233-9780. Or call Jacqueline Fraser (212-696-8388) or Lori Pepe (212-696-8297).

Basic Training

If your new dog is fully grown, it is probably housebroken, and, with any luck, has been taught how to behave. If not, don't worry: you can teach an old dog new tricks. If your new dog is a puppy, you certainly have your work cut out for you.

The first thing you need to decide is how you are going to train the dog. Are you going to do it yourself? Will you enroll Sparky in dog-training classes, or do you want private lessons? No matter what type of training you decide on, you must be committed to at least ten minutes of homework every day. Just going to class and listening to the teacher doesn't work unless you follow up at home.

If you have the discipline to be firm, understanding, and consistent with your dog, you can train the dog yourself. Some recommended books on the subject:

Colflesh, Linda, *Making Friends: Training Your Dog Positively* (Macmillan)

Davis, Kathy Diamond, *Responsible Dog Ownership* (Howell Book House)

Evans, Job Michael, *Civilized City Canines* (Howell Book House)

Kovary, Robin, *Good Puppy: How to Raise, Train and Protect the Puppy You Love* (Direct Book Service)

Pryor, Karen, *Don't Shoot The Dog!* (Bantam Books)

Rogerson, John, *Training Your Best Friend* (Howell Book House)

Woodhouse, Barbara, *No Bad Dogs The Woodhouse Way* (Summit Books)

If you decide to use a trainer, finding the right one is one of the most important dog decisions you will ever face. A good trainer will make your life much easier. A poor trainer will frustrate you and your dog and will end up wasting time and money.

Get recommendations from friends or neighbors with well-behaved dogs. Breeders and vets are other good sources. Your neighborhood pet supply and food store is also likely to know the trainers in your area. For a more formal referral, contact the Society of North American Dog Trainers (212-243-7862). Since anyone can call himself or herself a dog trainer, this group has created a certification testing program and developed a code of ethics.

The society suggests asking the following questions when considering a trainer:

- How many years of experience does the trainer have?

- What experience does the trainer have with your breed of dog and its problems?

- What are the costs involved?

- How far away are the classes?

- Does the trainer use a humane approach?

❖ If group classes are involved, how large is the group?

Group classes, usually less expensive than private ones, allow your dog to be socialized in class, and are especially helpful with young puppies, who may not yet be spending much time around other dogs and strangers. Your dog will learn to pay attention to you even if other dogs around want to play. Make sure classes are nearby; if it takes half an hour to get there, you and your dog may be tempted to play hookey on a rainy day.

The greatest advantage to private classes is that you and your dog have the trainer's undivided attention. Classes can be arranged to fit your schedule and can be held at home so the trainer can work with the dog in its own environment.

You can also have your dog trained at a boarding school. Bubba goes off for a week or more on his own to get the basics, and then the trainer will follow up with the two of you together.

Training styles range from outright force to kindly motivational training, as well as combinations of the two. Find out whether the trainer's approach and philosophy mesh with your own. (Do you simply want a well behaved pet

·that's a joy to be around, or are you interested in extensive obedience training so you can compete in obedience trials?) Ask questions and assume nothing. Before enrolling, request to see a class in progress. Any reputable trainer should be willing to accommodate you.

The city has hundreds of trainers of all types. Here is a sampling:

ASPCA
424 East 92nd Street
212-876-7700

Under training director Jacque Schultz, the basic eight-week course meets one hour a week (the first week is a lecture). Classes usually consist of five to eight owners and dogs. *Cost:* $230.

KEVIN BEHAN/CANINE ARTS
519 Federal Road
Brookefield, CT 06804
203-775-4404

Behan's six-week boarding/training program is recommended for problem dogs. For the first three weeks, your dog works alone with the trainer; during the second three weeks, you make repeated visits to learn how to work with the dog. If you don't want or need such intensive training, Saturday lessons are available. Behan also teaches private classes in Manhattan at No Standing Anytime, 414 East 73rd Street (212-472-0694). *Cost:* $1,600 for full program (includes all boarding fees).

BIDE-A-WEE
410 East 38th Street
212-532-4455

Group sessions are open to all dogs, regardless of whether or not they were adopted from Bide-a-Wee. A seven-session course for beginners usually takes six to eight owner/dog teams. *Cost:* $215.

CANINE COMPANION DOG TRAINING
212-243-5460

Robin Kovary, one of the founders of the Society of North American Dog Trainers, has been training dogs for over twelve years. A certified canine good citizenship evaluator, Kovary believes that training should be fun for both you and your dog, and her wide variety of programs for every budget emphasizes positive motivational training. Private lessons are customized to the needs of you and your dog and take place in your home and around your neighborhood. She covers puppy training, problem correction, obedience training, and can even train dogs for work with pet therapists. Semi-private lessons are also available. *Cost:* varies widely with packages for every need and budget; special discount for adopted, spayed, and neutered dogs.

THE EDUCATED PUPPY
718-788-3602

Bobbi Giella considers herself a combination companion, social worker, instructor, and canine psychologist. The emphasis in her Brooklyn and Manhattan training programs is on the new dog or puppy (you can call for a pre-purchase consultation). Her special "puppy package" consists of an at-home session with you and the puppy that covers feeding, housing, and parenting, followed by six group classes for socialization and further training. Giella also deals with behavioral problem solving for older dogs. *Cost:* $400 for puppy package, plus a strong telephone support system. Cost of other services varies.

FOLLOW MY LEAD
212-243-5460

Run by three women who see dog training as preventive maintenance. Puppy lessons emphasizing no-bite, noncompetitive play can begin as early as eight weeks. Courses beyond puppy training and obedience training include lessons in agility and dog tricks. *Cost:* $80 for individual lessons; $225 for a series of eight group lessons.

JIM KEENAN
800-237-3743

In addition to his group classes at Bide-a-Wee (see page 32), Keenan also offers private at-home lessons in Manhattan, Brooklyn, and Queens. Using motivational methods, he tailors the classes to your dog's disposition and personality. Personal protection training is available on a select basis. *Cost:* varies depending on services chosen.

PROSPECT PARK DOG TRAINING
718-499-4851

Run by Lori Sash Gail, editor of *Trainer's Forum*, a newsletter for animal trainers, and Bobbi Giella (see the Educated Puppy, above), this is the only year-round formal group class in Brooklyn. The emphasis is on kindly behavioral management. Both instructors are present at all times. *Cost:* $225 for a series of eight group sessions.

VANCOUVER DOG TRAINING SCHOOL
120 Riverside Drive
212-877-7116

Run by Pat McGregor, who has owned the school for the past nine years, Vancouver offers individual lessons and group classes, both of which emphasize humane training. Lessons for all levels and situations include new puppy training, show work, problem dogs, and pet-therapist certification. They will even help you find the right dog for you, from a purebred to a rescued mutt. *Cost:* varies widely, but no one will be turned away because of an inability to pay.

JANE WEINER
212-877-9484

Weiner specializes in training your dog at home, with the entire family participating. Her work on basic obedience, temperament training, and behavioral problems stresses respect, kindness, and clarity.

Good Grooming

Having your dog groomed professionally is a little like going to a hair salon. You can shampoo, set, and even cut your own hair if you have to, but when you want to look your best, you go to a professional.

The city has hundreds of groomers to choose from. Some vets employ groomers. Pet shops often have grooming facilities on their premises. Many kennels groom dogs. You can even have a groomer come to you.

Groomers aren't just for high-fashion cuts and styling. They're also ideal for giving a flea and tick dip, thorough shampoo, and nail clipping. At most groomers, you must make your appointment in advance.

Different groomers have different approaches. They can use tranquilizers or other types of restraints. Some specialize in herbal baths, while others are expert stylists. Once you decide what you want, ask for recommendations. If you are using a groomer for the first time, make sure you like what one or two "done" dogs look like before you leave yours.

The Manhattan grooming services listed below are a sampling of the different types throughout the city:

BEVERLY HILLS LAUNDER MUTT
45 Grove Street
212-691-7700

This friendly neighborhood shop offers self-service washtubs for you to wash your dog yourself if you don't have the facilities to do it at home. They supply everything but the dog, and prices start at $10. You can also make an appointment for a complete grooming; stay with your dog, or relax with a cup of coffee in the garden while Digger is having his bath. Their motto: "Treat the animal with love and kindness." Pickup and delivery services are available.

CREATURE FEATURES
3 Great Jones Street
212-473-5992

Services range from a simple nail trim to a full wash, cut, brush, and fluff for every type of dog, and the groomers are very knowledgeable about skin conditions. Grooming prices start at $25. Pickup and delivery available.

DOGGIE-DO & PUSSYCATS TOO
230 East 29th Street
212-679-7888

This full-service salon handles all breeds of dogs and offers grooming services including hand scissoring, hand stripping (if you have to ask, it's not for you), flea and tick dips, and medicated baths. Complete grooming treatments (including a haircut) start at $50. Pickup and delivery service available.

KAREN'S
1195 Lexington Avenue
212-472-9440

One of the largest salons in the city, Karen's employs seven groomers. They will do any breed of dog, and are especially well-known for their work with West Highland terriers. It's one of the few places in the city that still does hand stripping. A complete grooming session averages around $70.

LEE DAY
201-748-6420

Known as "the celebrity dog groomer," Day accompanies her in-home grooming services with a serenade of Broadway hits. A complete grooming/singing session in Manhattan starts at $65, including parking. With the aim of bringing love to pets and owners all over the tristate area, Day will arrange romantic dates for spayed or neutered dogs. She also conducts doggie weddings and even performed a "bark Mitzvah" for Joan Rivers' dog Spike.

SUTTON DOG PARLOUR
311 East 60th Street
212-355-2850

After grooming dogs for more than twenty years, owner Marcia Habib says there's nothing she can't do or hasn't already done. Grooming is done in full public view, but Habib requests that the owner remain outside the grooming room itself. Prices start at $40 depending on the size of the dog and the type of coat.

Keeping the City Dog Safe

Although city streets are free of wild animals who might pounce on your dog, dangers lurk, nevertheless, and vigilance is a must. A few tips on keeping your dog out of harm's way:

❖ Be sure your dog is vaccinated against rabies.

❖ Keep a list of emergency phone numbers (vet, poison control, etc.) by the phone.

❖ Get a decal or sign for your door that

informs firemen of your dog's presence in case of a fire.

❖ Take a choke or pinch collar off when your dog is unattended at home.

❖ Avoid tying your dog outside a store for even a few minutes. Dogs are often stolen.

❖ Always keep ID and license tags on—it's the best way to ensure that your dog will be returned if he or she gets loose.

❖ Watch out for things dogs love—rotten meat, chicken bones, mystery meat—in the street.

❖ Stop your male dog from urinating on metal lampposts. He can be electrocuted if electrical fixtures are open or exposed.

❖ Keep your dog away from any area that has recently been exterminated. Sprays and poisons that are used to control pests such as roaches and rats may also harm dogs. Even in the best building, beware of rat poison in basements, garages, and courtyards. If the laundry facilities are in the basement, leave your dog in the apartment on wash day.

Keeping the City Dog Safe

- Close, bar, or screen all accessible windows. Dogs don't have nine lives.

- Guard against frostbite and hypothermia in winter. If your dog is shivering or shaking, get inside as quickly as possible. And treat him to a winter coat.

- Check foot pads on all four paws for frostbite and salt accumulation. Before venturing out, cover them with petroleum jelly or invest in a set of dog boots.

- Stay away from antifreeze spills in the street. The stuff tastes nice and sweet, but it's deadly.

- Watch out for the heat, and make sure plenty of fresh water for drinking is available in summer.

- Beware of fireworks. Dogs develop noise phobias easily. If you're in a potentially noisy area, close the windows, and block the sound by putting on the air conditioner and the radio. Better yet, wrangle an out-of-town invitation for the two of you.

- Keep your home as cool as possible. If it's very hot, keep the air conditioner going or set up a fan safely out of the dog's reach. Dogs with pushed-in noses such as bulldogs and pugs are especially susceptible to heat stress.

❖ Keep cleaning supplies and other toxic substances out of the dog's reach.

❖ Make sure there are no exposed wires around, and don't let any dog chew on electrical cords.

❖ No bones. Chicken, lamb chop, and veal bones can all splinter. If you must, use beef marrow bones. Your best bet: a rawhide bone from the pet supply shop.

❖ Keep your Hershey bars to yourself. To dogs, chocolate can be poison.

Dog Runs

In New York City, it's illegal to let your dog run off the leash. The law exists not only to protect others, but also to protect your dog. On a leash, it can't run away.

The city opened its first official enclosed dog run in Manhattan's Tompkins Square Park in 1990 after park users complained that dogs were pawing and ruining the grass. Since then several other official runs have opened in Manhattan, making dog owners and park users equally happy. Although informal dog runs are scattered throughout the city (especially in the parks), it's a good idea to use a formal dog run if you live near one. Your dog will love it, and you won't have to worry that your best friend will run away.

A word of caution: Remove the choke collar whenever you let your dog run free to play with other dogs. If the collar gets caught on another dog's collar or tags, it becomes almost impossible to separate the two dogs. The results can be disastrous (they don't call it a choke collar for nothing).

Leave the flat collar with the dog's ID tags on. Not only does it provide identification, it also gives you something to hold if you have to grab your dog suddenly.

Some of the formal dog runs in Manhattan include:

BATTERY PARK CITY DOG RUN
West Street below Chambers Street

This long, narrow, enclosed asphalt run is located along the West Side Highway, adjacent to Battery Park City. Although privately organized, it's open to the public and offers some shade from the park's trees. *Amenities:* breezes, Hudson River views, romping under the watchful eye of the Statue of Liberty.

Dog Runs

WASHINGTON SQUARE PARK DOG RUN
Fifth Avenue below 8th Street

This highly organized dirt-and-wood-chip run may be the most popular run in the city. Signs posted state the rules: Dogs must be innoculated, healthy, and parasite-free; no aggressive dogs or dogs in heat; no people without dogs. As crowded as the run can get, especially on nice weekends, it is kept amazingly clean by a poop patrol. *Amenities:* plenty of romping space for the dogs; lots of benches, trees, and shade for the owners.

LAGUARDIA PLACE DOG RUN
Mercer and Houston Streets
212-505-0304

You need a key to get into this limited-admission club. Not run by the Parks Department, the run has a waiting list (just like a good private school). Some folks tout this long, narrow asphalt surface as the best run in the city. It is very clean, but to us it's barren and boring. *Amenities:* a hose with running water and a children's plastic swimming pool for the dogs.

THEODORE ROOSEVELT PARK DOG RUN
Museum of Natural History
Columbus Avenue and 81st Street

At this spacious enclosed dirt run, there is a separate area for small dogs and puppies. Toys and balls are allowed in this popular, friendly place, and you can always find a few old tennis balls lying around for an impromptu toss. *Amenities:* shade trees and benches. However, there is no running water, so on a hot summer day thirsty pups should bring their own.

RIVERSIDE PARK
Riverside Drive between 72nd and 122nd Streets

Although most of Riverside Park is an informal dog run, there are enclosed areas at Eighty-Seventh and One Hundred and Sixth Streets.

CARL SCHURTZ PARK DOG RUN
85th Street and York Avenue

A well-maintained enclosed run with a clean, elegant, pebbled surface worthy of the Upper East Side. The picturesque setting is shaded with trees and furnished with benches. *Amenities:* park rest rooms with running water for thirsty pets.

J. HOOD WIRTH PARK DOG RUN
Fort Washington Avenue and 173rd Street

This run is enclosed, dirt-surfaced, and pooch friendly.

TOMPKINS SQUARE PARK DOG RUN
10th Street and Avenue A

This nice, large, enclosed dirt run surrounded by basketball courts and playgrounds has a real community feel. To prevent fights, no dogs in heat are allowed; no balls, Frisbees, or toys either. One other rule: "Humans also expected to behave inoffensively." *Amenities:* large shade trees, benches, and running water in the surrounding park.

Dogs Allowed/
No Dogs Allowed

Wouldn't it be great if we could take our dogs everywhere? Wouldn't it be nice to walk the dog and do errands at the same time? Unfortunately, in New York City it simply isn't possible.

Certain establishments don't allow dogs, and they include supermarkets, delis, vegetable stores, fish markets—any place that serves or sells food. This isn't a decision made by the proprietors, but a law enforced by the city. Resist the temptation to tie Coco up outside a store while you "just run in for a loaf of bread." Dogs do get stolen and can also get loose and run off.

Unlike the French, New Yorkers can't even think about taking their dogs into restaurants. The closest the two of you can come to having a meal out together is getting a hot dog in the park or finding a sympathetic outdoor café or restaurant.

Do everyone a favor: If your dog is not well-behaved, don't take it into any store.

❖ If a store has a "No Dogs Allowed" sign, respect the owner's wishes.

❖ Never leave your dog tied up outside a store alone.

Bookstores, however, are a great place to take a well-behaved dog. Here is a sampling of Manhattan bookstores that recognize that browsing and dog walking go together:

BARNES AND NOBLE (SUPER) STORES
Citywide

This chain used to welcome dogs with open paws. But those with new cafés slip into the food-serving category, and the pooches have to go.

B. DALTON
396 Sixth Avenue and 8th Street

An unhesitating "yes."

COLISEUM BOOKS
1771 Broadway

Dogs allowed, but very large dogs discouraged. There isn't much room in the aisles.

THE CORNER BOOKSTORE
1313 Madison Avenue

One of the dog friendliest stores in town. They keep a supply of biscuits on hand, throw welcome-back parties when summer vacations are over, and celebrate other noteworthy dog occasions.

DOUBLEDAY
724 Fifth Avenue

Only allows dogs with good manners.

ENDICOTT BOOKSELLERS
450 Columbus Avenue

Any dog you can carry.

MADISON AVENUE BOOK SHOP
833 Madison Avenue

A very firm "of course."

MURDER INK
2486 Broadway

The perfect store for the dog who likes mysteries.

SHAKESPEARE AND COMPANY
716 Broadway

2259 Broadway

Both locations are dog friendly, but if the store is very crowded and your dog is very large, the manager might ask the two of you to stay near the door while someone else fetches your book.

THE STRAND
828 Broadway

Another very dog friendly shop.

And Devoted Exclusively to Dog Lovers and Their Dogs...

DOG LOVERS BOOKSHOP
9 West 31st Street
Second Floor
212-594-3601

If you're looking for a book about dogs—any book—this is the place. They carry all the current books, both fiction and nonfiction, and an extensive line of out-of-print and antiquarian books. You can also find a wide assortment of note cards, posters, rubber stamps, and other dog-related stationary items here. Owners Bern Marcowitz and Margot Rosenberg put a water bowl out to welcome dogs.

Dog Clothes

Although dogs come equipped with their own coats, they aren't all made for New York City's variable climate. For the times when nature needs to be helped, we have doggie clothes: coats, sweaters, boots, raincoats, formal wear, and Santa outfits. Leashes from plain cloth to hand-tooled leather, collars, as well as personalized bowls, beds, and toys are also available.

Stores

The Manhattan boutiques listed below suggest the variety and scope of items for your dog:

CANINE STYLES
830 Lexington Avenue
212-751-4549

Good quality coats, leads, leashes, and beds, and more can be found here.

DOGGIE-DO AND PUSSYCATS TOO
230 East 29th Street
212-679-7888

This boutique specializes in custom-made coats and sweaters. Their designers will also whip up formal wear (tuxedos or ball gowns) to match your favorite dress, suit, or tie, or make any one-of-a-kind garment you can think of. You name it and they make it, so long as "it isn't harmful to the dog."

DUDLEY'S PAW
327 Greenwich Street
212-966-5167

Handmade sweaters start here at $40. Orders for custom colors, designs, and sizes will be filled if your dog can't be fitted "off the rack." Check out the backpacks that allow your dog to carry a stock of personal supplies.

Dog Clothes

IT'S A DOG'S LIFE
239 West 72nd Street
212-875-9662

Everything is available here, from sweaters and books
to leashes and general supplies.

KAREN'S FOR PEOPLE AND PETS
1195 Lexington Avenue
212-472-9440

Karen designs and sells beautiful sweaters and coats
for dogs. The shop also carries its own brand of dog
cologne.

PET DEPARTMENT STORE
233 West 54th Street
212-498-9195

This store carries a very large selection of clothes for
all types of dogs and occasions. Also available is a wide
range of costumes for Halloween or any other time
your dog wants to look exotic.

Mail Order

Several specialty companies have outstanding
selections of coats, collars, and leashes to
order. Call for a catalog or brochure.

ALPINE PET SUPPLY
955 Massachusetts Avenue
P.O. Box 9183
Cambridge, MA 02139
800-242-7463

This is a good source for no-nonsense collars and leads. Their products are made of vegetable-tanned french leather, saddle-stitched, hand finished, oiled, and waterproofed, with mountaineering-gauge solid brass fittings. Collar prices start at $40. Special find: The Alpine sporting lead can be worn across your shoulder to free your hands for packages. Great for errands.

KLEIN DESIGNS, INC.
P.O. Box 417
Glenshaw, PA 15116
412-486-3094

Check out their K-Kollar, a heavy collar made with a double strand of chain.

WE SET THE STANDARD
1120 West Addison Street
Chicago, IL 60613
312-327-2201

This company offers a distinguished selection of leather collars, leashes, leads, harnesses, name plates, and tags. The few classic coats include raincoats and a super-warm topcoat. Everything is high quality; nothing is cutesy.

The Dog as Art

Do you want a wonderful pet portrait to put on a Christmas card or to give as a birthday present? It can be done. Just as some artists and photographers specialize in children, others have the good sense to specialize in pets.

Here are some places that can immortalize your dog in one medium or another:

JUDITH GWYN BROWN
522 East 85th Street
212-288-1599

Judith Gwyn Brown, a children's book author, specializes in dog portraits. She will paint the dog alone or with its owner. She works from photographs and she also looks at the dog. Her watercolors and oils are done in the traditional eighteenth- and nineteenth-century style, and she can place your dog in any setting from the living room couch to Central Park to a bucolic field. Watercolors are $600 for a fourteen-by-seventeen portrait; oils start at $1,000 for the same size.

CREATURE COMFORTS
P.O. Box 606
Vashon, WA 98070

A hand spinner will turn dog combings into soft, lovely yarns, garments, and blankets. Send a self-addressed, stamped envelope for more information.

FUR FACES
212-929-2430

Therese Cannon-King, who lives with two dogs and four cats that she has rescued, and her partner Nym Bjorkland, photograph your dog in your home. They feel it's the best place to capture the animal's true personality. Prices start at $295.

S. G. HOFFMAN
42 Gabriel Road
Cochecton, NY 12726
914-583-6315

Send several photographs (different angles) along with your pet's name, and receive a hand-sculpted, hand-painted statue. Sculptures are about seven inches high if the animal is sitting, or six inches long laying down.

The Dog as Art

All come on a wooden base. Mutts are welcome.
Starting at $49.95.

JOAN'S NEEDLECRAFT STUDIO
240 East 29th Street
212-532-7129

Bring a photograph of your dog to the studio, and an
artist will paint it onto a needlepoint canvas for you to
stitch up. For an additional fee, someone will even
complete the project for you. The price is about $125.

MABEL'S
849 Madison Avenue
212-734-3263

One of the city's best stores for dog artifacts. Portraits
can be done in watercolor, pen and ink, or oils on an
eight-inch round canvas. An unequalled treasure, a
hand-hooked rug with an image of your dog looking up
at you, can also be ordered here. Portraits start at $50;
special-order rugs begin at $725.

THE MASTER'S TOUCH ART STUDIO
800-325-0561

Illinois-based Karen Dummenil works from photographs (you must provide them) to capture your dog
using "old masters' techniques." Watercolors and pencil
sketches start at $100; oil, pastel, and colored-pencil
portraits begin at $140.

MIMI VANG OLSEN
545 Hudson Street
212-675-5410

Mimi Vang Olsen does beautiful realistic oil portraits. She goes to your home and takes photographs of your dog and then paints a magnificent likeness against a mutually agreed upon background—anything from the living room couch to a field of wildflowers. It takes two to three months to complete a portrait, and she is only available October though May. Prices start at $3,000.

PAULETTE SINCLAIR
60 West 8th Street
212-533-4208

Sinclair photographs your dog at home or in her studio, whichever you prefer. Her motto is: "I picture your pet as a work of art." Prices start at $120.

PAW PRINTS
46 Cooper Lane
Larchmont, NY 10538
914-834-9029

Dog photography by Tata Darling. Original watercolor portraits can also be done here.

PET FUZZIES
25325 Southeast 133rd Road
Issaquah, WA 98027

Laurie Nix will spin your dog's hair (don't try this with a short-haired breed) into a "wearable keepsake." For information, send a self-addressed, stamped envelope.

PETOGRAPHY
25 Central Park West
Suite 3A
212-245-0914

The Dog as Art

Jim Dratfield and Paul Couglin like to photograph your dog wherever he or she is most comfortable—at home or at their studio, indoors or out. Known for their sepia-toned Victorian look, they also work in black and white. (Their photographs often show up on the cover of *Pethouse* magazine.) The price for one framed and two matted photographs is $325; $25 of the fee goes to the animal cause of your choice. Note cards and postcards are also available.

PET PORTRAITS BY ANNIE
RFD 2, Box 185
Tilton, NH 03276
603-524-3778

If you send Annie a color photograph and a short personality description, she promises that her painting will "capture your pet's love and friendship on canvas." Prices start at $62.50.

PRISCILLA SNYDER
212-344-2209

She will make a beautiful custom-made tapestry shoulder bag featuring a likeness of your dog. She can also create a life-like cloth sculpture from six inches high to life-size, or larger. She works from photographs.

SANDRA PELUSO
800-901-0505

Working from color photographs she takes herself, Peluso creates distinguished oil portraits of your dog alone or with you.

Dog Psychics

Do you want to communicate with your dog through a medium? Look into the crystal ball and find out what Bubba's future holds? Read Rover's tarot cards? It can be done.

Here are some sources to consider:

THE ANIMAL PSYCHIC
P.O. Box 1374
New York, NY 10028

If you send a picture of your pet and three questions, this psychic will use tarot cards, astrology, numerology, and runes to answer them. Necessary for the reading are: the dog's date of birth, breed, sex, name, and $40. The picture will be returned.

CRYSTAL ENERGY
304 West 11th Street
212-229-0697

Kim Demetro does readings for people and for dogs. Just bring in your pet, his collar, or a picture. A full-life reading tells you the dog's past, present, and future: Should she have pups? How long will he live? What makes her nervous? A half-life reading deals strictly with the present. Call for an appointment. Full-life readings are $50; half-life readings are $25.

DAWN HAYMAN
Spring Farm Cares
3364 State Route 12
Clinton, NY 13323
315-737-9339

Dawn Hayman is an animal communications consultant. She considers herself a link between owners and animals, and her goal is to teach the owner how to communicate telepathically with the animal. You can call her with behavioral problems, or if your dog seems depressed or just out of sorts. The dog does not have to be present when you call, since telepathy doesn't know time or space. Or you can attend one of her workshops, which will teach you how to communicate with your dog. Phone calls are $25 for twenty minutes; $40 for a half hour. Workshops start at $125; call or write for times and locations.

 61

Getting it by Mail

Even though we live in a city where there's a store for everything, shopping by catalog for pet supplies is very appealing. If you love getting packages in the mail and want to share that thrill with your dog, call one of the places listed below for a free catalog.

CHERRYBROOK
P.O. Box 15, Route 57
Broadway, NJ 08808
800-524-0820

Shampoos and grooming supplies, crates, beds, and pillows are featured here. An older or sick dog might appreciate a Pet-O-Pedic mattress, designed to relieve pressure on joints and injuries. From $15.95. Rawhide bakery treats—a bagel or a croissant—are $1.95. Now you and the dog can have breakfast together.

DOCTORS FOSTER AND SMITH, INC.
2253 Air Park Road
P.O. Box 100
Rhinelander, WI 54501
800-826-7206

This veterinarian-owned and operated company offers beds, healthcare products, sanitary pads, and pants, including gingham-ruffled Doggie Britches by Dottie from $5.99. Treats include a make-your-own dog biscuit mix complete with a bone-shaped cookie cutter for $6.99. Sweatshirts, sweaters, training devices, and a large selection of books are also available.

J. B. WHOLESALE PET SUPPLIES, INC.
5 Raritan Road
Oakland, NJ 07436
800-526-0388

Just about everything you might need, from seventy kinds of grooming shears to a wide assortment of balls, is available here. There is even a sleeping bag so your dog can enjoy a cozy, draft-free nap. Starting at $16.95.

PEDIGREES
1918 Transit Way
Box 905
Brockport, NY 14420
800-548-4786

This place sells great toys and accessories. If your dog never learned the dog paddle, invest in a soft vinyl, adjustable life preserver. In six sizes starting at $29.99. And what dog doesn't need a studded "leather" biker jacket? Washable. $49.99.

PET WAREHOUSE
Box 310
Xenia, OH 45385
800-443-1160

This is a good source for toys, grooming supplies, ear wipes, lots of odor and stain removers, and a large assortment of food and clothes. Beds include Autoloo by Dogloo, a car-shaped dream machine that costs $21.44 and is bound to convince any apartment-bound dog that he's out on the road. A Groom 'N' Vac attachment that fits most vacuum cleaners and removes loose hair from your pet is $9.19.

R. C. STEELE
1989 Transit Way
Brockport, NY 14420
800-872-3773

Featured here are pet equipment and kennel supplies, collars, leads, pooper scoopers, training aids, shampoos, and grooming towels. Collars monogrammed with your dog's name and phone number are $12.98. If you've done your apartment in fifties style, a brightly colored anodized aluminum dog bowl ($1.98 and up) will fit right in. Special doggie Frisbees with a hambone scent or chocolate-caramel flavor start at $2.47. For the gourmet dog: hickory-smoked pig ears that are "chewy, tasty, and smoked to bring out that great rich pork flavor."

Caregivers

Walkers, Sitters, and Kennels

In order to pay for dog food and doggie toys, most New York City dog owners have to go out and earn a living. They can't stay home all day to care for the dog's every need. However, they can always arrange for someone who can. Remember to always leave your veterinarian's name with any walkers, sitters, kennels, or friends who might be taking care of your pet.

Dog Walkers

Dog walkers come to your home during the day and walk your dog for fifteen minutes to an hour; the arrangement is up to you. Dog walkers range from highly organized professionals to the kid in the apartment next door. Since the walker will not only be taking care of your pet, but will also have the key to your apartment, honesty is of primary importance. You don't want to come home and find both your dog and your television missing. Reliability is as important as honesty. Your dog will not understand if the walker doesn't show up because of a toothache. To find a reliable walker in your neighborhood, ask your vet, the local pet store owner, friends and neighbors. Request, and check references. Here are some names to get you started:

DOGGIE NANNY
212-249-0877

Individual dog walking or sitting in your home. Half hour walks start at $9; hour walks at $13. There is a $1 premium if you live above the second floor in a walk-up. Nanny can stay overnight in your home for $33; $38 on holidays.

FURRY TAILS
212-938-TAIL

Monica Diaz and her husband Bradley run this family-owned business that walks dogs who live between Sixtieth and Ninetieth streets on the East Side, and in Forest Hills and Jackson Heights, Queens. An individual half-hour walk is $10, or you can have a two-hour group walk with four to eight other dogs for $12. If you have a new puppy who gets lonely, they will also pay house visits, play with and feed the puppy, and keep it company for a half-hour.

NOAH'S ARK
4414 Sixth Avenue
Brooklyn
718-871-7685

This bonded and insured company serves Park Slope, Cobble Hill, and Brooklyn Heights, and prides itself on being very neighborhood oriented. Dogs are walked individually for twenty minutes or more with prices starting at $10. If you have to go out of town and don't want to put Fido in a kennel, pet sitters are available.

PET GET-A-WAY
212-534-7924

Individual dog walking or a prearranged play date can be made with another dog in most areas of Manhattan. Only one dog (or one household's dogs) are cared for at a time. Walks, with the dog always on the leash, are a half-hour or longer and start at $15. Member of the National Association of Professional Pet Sitters.

POWARS (Pet Owners with AIDS Resource Services)

P.O. Box 1116
Madison Square Station, NY 10159
212-744-0842

This organization is dedicated to helping people with AIDS take care of their pets: Volunteers will feed and walk dogs and take them to the vet.

VANCOUVER DOG TRAINING SCHOOL

120 Riverside Drive
212-877-7116

This training school also provides individual dog walking services with the utmost care and consideration. Walks are for a half-hour or more.

Dog Sitters/Kennels

If Fido wants more than a walk while you're out earning money for dog biscuits, send him to *day care*. This usually takes place in a kennel-like setting where your dog gets to play with other dogs, gets walked, gets fed, and has an all-around good time. Manhattan choices include:

CANINE COUNTRY

207 West 75th Street
212-877-7777

This day-care program with general kennel facilities and a play area operates from 8:30 A.M. to 6:30 P.M. If you get held up at the office, you can make special arrangements to pick up your dog until 10 P.M. *Cost:* $15 a day; boarding is $24 a day.

NO STANDING ANY TIME
414 East 73rd Street
212-472-0694

Just like nursery school with walks five or six times a day, playtime, quiet time, and cookie time. You can also arrange for grooming. *Cost:* $30 a day which includes pickup and drop off.

PETSUPERETTE
187 East 93rd Street
212-534-1732

From 8:30 A.M. until 6:00 P.M., your dog will get walked and have a chance to play with other dogs. He or she will be fed; special diets can be accommodated if you bring the food. *Cost:* from $15 a day. Pickup and delivery service available.

YUPPIE PUPPY PET CARE
274 West 86th Street
212-887-2747

Another "nursery school," with an indoor playroom and an outdoor backyard available from 8 A.M. to 7:45 P.M. You also can arrange for your dog to attend play sessions or an obedience class during the day. *Cost:* from $10 a day; overnight boarding from $30.

Long-term care

If you have to spend time away from home and can't take the dog with you (let's say your boss doesn't want a lovable mutt at the next sales conference in Miami), then arrangements need to be made. You can send the dog to a kennel in the city or the country, or you can even hire someone to come and sit for Dina in your own apartment. Some of your choices are:

CUSTOMIZED PET SERVICES
718-956-5598

Along with Mr. and Mrs. Robert Douek and their grade-school son, your dog will have the run of an entire house in Astoria, Queens. Since the Doueks never take more than two or three dogs at a time, excellent attention is given to all your dog's needs. Long-term stays can be arranged. Owners are welcome to call in and check on their pets; calls have come from as far away as Hong Kong and Bali. *Cost:* $35 a night, plus $25 for pickup.

THE MALIBU PET HOTEL
107 Guy Lombardo Avenue
Freeport, Long Island
212-432-6800

Facilities include runs, doggie apartments, kennels (all under twenty-four-hour supervision) as well as grooming and training. Their motto is "Loving, Confidence, Patience." *Cost:* from $20 with pickup and delivery.

Caregivers

PAWS INN
189 Ninth Avenue
212-645-7279

370 West 35th Street
212-736-PAWS

Both locations offer twenty four-hour supervision. "Guests" stay in little open rooms furnished with couches and chairs that create a homey feeling. They can sun and play on the roof deck and are walked three or four times a day. Day-care is also available from 7 A.M. to 7 P.M. *Cost:* $35 a night with a 10% discount for four or more days; day-care is $20 a day.

QUIN KAH WOL KENNELS
Stoneridge, NY 12484
914-687-7619

This kennel is located in a beautiful Catskill setting and is run by three women who used to work for the ASPCA in Manhattan. Under twenty-four-hour supervision, the dogs stay, not in cages, but in indoor and outdoor runs with classical music playing in the background. Facilities include a special exercise area, and you can arrange for training and basic grooming during your dog's stay. *Cost:* $15 a day. Pickup and delivery can be arranged.

RAVENWOOD KENNEL
Middletown, NY
914-386-2677

A little over an hour from the city, this kennel features
both heat and central air-conditioning and has sixty
outdoor and indoor runs, as well as a large exercise
area to keep the dogs active. If Fred is used to running
around and playing with other dogs, he'll be allowed off
the leash. If Max is more comfortable being walked,
he'll be walked on the leash. The dogs get a daily
yogurt snack and a chance to participate in Nerf foot-
ball games. A veterinarian is on call around the clock,
and someone is always on the premises. Owner Sara
Whalen specializes in geriatric dogs and dogs who don't
get along well with other dogs. Grooming is available.
Cost: Prices start at $18 a day, full American plan, with
no charge for medication. Pickup and delivery can be
arranged starting at $35 per round-trip.

Supply and Food Shops

Having a good pet supply shop nearby makes it easier to be a good pet owner. Most people who work in these stores love animals and are happy to answer all your questions. Along with your dog food, you can often pick up the name of a reliable dog walker or veterinarian. We've developed what we call the "bulletin board theory": if there is a bulletin board displayed prominently and it is full of notices and pictures of lost and found neighborhood dogs and cats, you know you are in good hands.

With nearly one hundred pet stores in Manhattan alone, it would be impossible to list every shop in the city. Here, however, is a smattering of what's around:

Bronx

ANIMAL FEEDS
3255 Park Avenue
718-293-7750

At the same site for fifty-six years and in the same family for three generations, this former horse-and-chicken-feed store now caters to house pets. The owners run behavioral clinics, offer training tips, and bring in vets to give $10 rabies shots six times a year. They also work with the Fund for Animals to encourage spaying and neutering, and carry a wide selection of harnesses and collars to fit the area's large dogs. Closed Sundays.

Brooklyn

MOTHER'S
370 Seventh Avenue
718-788-8688

This is a good neighborhood store in Park Slope. Come here for free food to start you off if you've rescued a dog, as well as referrals for placement, rescue, walking, and transportation services. They carry a large selection of food, leashes, and toys. Open seven days a week.

Manhattan

ANIMAL HOUSE
549 Ninth Avenue
212-757-2924

This store offers grooming services, a solid selection of foods, and all accessories. Free local delivery. Open seven days.

ANIMAL WORLD
21 East 26th Street
212-685-0027

This shop carries "everything but the animal." Special orders including prescription foods are welcome, and UPS shipping is available. Stop in for referrals and adoption information. Delivery available. Closes Sundays.

THE BARKING ZOO
172 Ninth Avenue
212-255-0658

238 Third Avenue
212-228-4848

Specializing in health food, these shops carry a full line of quality foods, accessories, and books. Their motto is "Your Pet Deserves the Best." Free local delivery. Open seven days.

BEASTY FEAST
237 Bleecker Street
212-243-3261

630 Hudson Street
212-620-7099

These stores are well stocked with food (some health food) and accessories, and are good sources for local referrals. Manhattan deliveries available. The Bleecker Street store is open seven days; the one on Hudson Street is closed Sundays.

CALLING ALL PETS
301 East 76th Street

1590 York Avenue
212-249-PETS (both stores)

The Pet Advantage Club here offers substantial savings and discounts. Free delivery. Open seven days.

CREATURE COMFORTS
2778 Broadway
212-864-9964

Carrying a full line of food and accessories, this friendly neighborhood store likes to be on a first-name basis with all dog and human customers. They offer referrals and answer telephone inquires when the store isn't crowded. Delivery is available. Open seven days.

CREATURE FEATURES
3 Great Jones Street
212-473-5992

All the standard brands of dog food are available here, as well as health foods, Abaday frozen foods, herbal supplements, and food for special body-building diets. Grooming and referrals are available. Deliveries in Manhattan. Closed Sundays.

DOG-O-RAMA
161 Seventh Avenue South
212-627-3647

A good assortment of food, accessories, and special-order clothes can be found here. Grooming and boarding for small dogs are available. Open seven days.

DUDLEY'S PAW
327 Greenwich Street
212-966-5167

This shop carries all premium brands of dog food, as well as toys, treats, beds, and bowls. Available by special order: hand-made dog sweaters. Free delivery service. Closed Sundays.

LITTLE ARF 'N ANNIE
458 Broome Street
212-431-1682

This is probably the only store in Manhattan that sells food for pets and people; all brands of dog food are carried, along with owner-type gourmet salads and goodies. A complete line of dog accessories is also featured. Delivery available. Open seven days.

LITTLE CREATURES
126 Saint Mark's Place
212-473-2857

770 Amsterdam Avenue
212-932-8610

Both stores carry prescription foods and specialize in health foods. They guarantee the lowest prices in town and will match or beat any other shop. Free delivery; $20 minimum. Open seven days.

PAMPERED PAWS
227 East 57th Street
212-935-PAWS

This shop carries a full line of premium dog foods, along with an extensive array of bowls, leashes, and grooming aids. And, as befits its location, the store calls itself "New York's Most Exclusive Upscale Dog and Cat Boutique." Free delivery throughout Manhattan and Roosevelt Island. Open seven days.

THE PET BAR
98 Thompson Street
212-274-0510

Food, health foods, loads of toys, and rawhide chews are the mainstays here. The large selection of hand-made leather collars and leashes include a collar with flashing lights so you (and passing cars) can see Rex at night. Free delivery. Open seven days.

THE PET BOWL
440 Amsterdam Avenue
212-580-2400

More than four hundred varieties of cat and dog food
are sold here, along with every accessory imaginable
from boots to beds. Excellent referral and support
information. Join the buyers' club for discounts. Free,
same-day delivery. Open seven days.

THE PET DEPARTMENT STORE
233 West 54th Street
212-489-9195

An enormous array of accessories and clothing, including costumes and Burberry-style raincoats, can be pur-
chased here. In addition, there is an extensive selection of books, as well as videos for rent and sale. This
store also features a holistic health clinic, and Lucy
can enjoy free use of treadmills. Open seven days.

PETER'S EMPORIUM FOR PETS
1449 Second Avenue
212-772-3647

This store offers a complete selection of dog food and
accessories. Free delivery. Open seven days.

PET NECESSITIES
236 East 75th Street
212-988-0769

This veterinarian-supervised shop carries a large selection of foods and accessories, including handmade
coats, sweaters, and bowls. Health and grooming supplies are also available. Delivery available; 50¢ charge.

PET'S KITCHEN
116 Christopher Street
212-242-3924

This shop carries a full selection of food and accessories. Special orders gladly filled. Free delivery. Open seven days until 10 P.M.

THE PET STOP
552 Columbus Avenue
212-580-2400

A wide assortment of food, clothes, toys, books, and more is featured here. Referral services available, as well as a discount pet food club. Convenient automatic delivery service; no charge for orders over $20. Open seven days.

WHISKERS
235 East 9th Street
800-WHISKERS

If you are interested in alternative dog care, this holistically oriented health food store is for you. They sell chemical-free food, vitamins and supplements, herbs, and flower remedies. They also hold regular workshops on related topics such as "Grooming and Natural Skin Care." The helpful staff will refer you to traditionally-trained holistic and homeopathic vets. For products and information on alternative dog care and a holistic life-style, this store is tops. Local deliveries and nationwide shipping service available. Open seven days.

Queens

K-9 CATERS
89-50 Metropolitan Avenue
Rego Park
718-275-5614

In business for twenty-six years, K-9 prides itself on its "wholesale prices for pet products." They carry a large assortment of foods and accessories that they will deliver throughout Queens and Brooklyn. Phone orders are welcome. Closed Sundays.

Deliveries

Most shops fill and deliver phone orders, and many even accept fax orders. If you have a large dog, or more than one dog, it's particularly convenient to be able to order by phone and spare yourself the trip and the lug.

A service that does nothing but home deliveries:

MR. B'S PET DEPOT
718-423-0082

Mr. B's delivers throughout Queens and Manhattan and is willing to beat any price in town. All food requests filled, including special prescriptions from your vet. As a bonus, this friendly, helpful service also delivers Deer Park bottled water. For you or your pampered pet? No questions asked.

Special Events

Special events that you and your dog can attend together range from blessings to fund-raisers to neighborhood gatherings. Here are some of the best-known:

ASPCA DOG WALK
Rumsey Field
Central Park
212-876-7700
Held at the end of October.

Affectionately known as "Woofstock," this is a real dog extravaganza with close to two thousand four-legged participants. There are one-, two-, or four-mile walks you can join and then a dog festival with Frisbee and obedience demonstrations, entertainment, live music, dog and people food, and dog and people celebrities.

THE BLESSING OF THE ANIMALS
Cathedral of Saint John the Divine
West 112th Street and Amsterdam Avenue
212-316-7400
Held the first Sunday in October.

A wonderful religious service with all animals welcome. If your pup goes wild at the sight of a duck or elephant, think twice before attending.

THE BLESSING OF THE ANIMALS
Prospect Park
718-965-8968
Held on St. Francis of Assisi Feast Day, October 4.

Animals of all sizes and shapes are welcome, and dogs seem to love it.

Note: Many Episcopal churches have a Blessing of the Animals service on St. Francis of Assisi Feast Day. Check with your local church to see if there is a service near you.

DACHSHUND FRIENDSHIP FEST
Washington Square Park
212-475-5512
Held in May and October.

Sponsored by the Dachshund Friendship Club (c/o Adrian Milton, 245 East 11th Street, N.Y., N.Y. 10003), this event features a meeting and march of dachshunds. The dogs and owners get to know each other, exchange information, make play dates, and celebrate the breed. A newsletter is also available.

K9 DAY
Hudson River Park
Gansevoort and West Streets
212-289-4113
Held in mid-May.

This benefit for the Humane Society of the United States includes a two-mile walk, agility demonstrations, a newspaper-fetching contest, prizes, and fun for the two-footed and the four-footed.

PAWS WALK AGAINST CANCER
89th Street and Riverside Drive
212-237-3872
Held in mid-May.

Organized by the American Cancer Society, this dog walk-a-thon raises money to fight both human and animal cancers with a portion of the proceeds going to the Animal Medical Center.

THE WESTMINSTER DOG SHOW
Madison Square Garden
212-696-8200
Held in February.

Run by the American Kennel Club, this is *the* dog show in the United States. If your dog is entered, he or she gets to go. Otherwise, this is a humans-only event. If you are considering getting a purebred, this is the best place to get a picture of the breed's potential and to meet breeders. If you already have a pedigreed dog, attend so you can see how Fifi measures up.

Taking a Trip

Transport

Transporting your dog without a car can be a problem. Taxis are fine for local trips if your dog is small and healthy, but getting a cab to take a dog who is large or ill isn't always easy. The solution is to call an animal transport service. (There have been some unfortunate incidents with dogs in airplanes, so if your dog must fly, investigate the carrier carefully before letting yours on board.) Here's a sampling of the local services:

BIG APPLE PET TAXI
718-965-4109

Primarily a Brooklyn operation, this company provides rides to and from the vet or the airport. *Cost:* Local Brooklyn trips start at $10; Brooklyn to JFK is around $40; Manhattan to JFK costs about $75.

METRO-NORTH COMMUTER RAILROAD
212-532-4900

This railroad allows dogs as long as they are well-behaved and on a leash. It's a great and inexpensive way to take Clara out for a day in the country. Your dog doesn't even need a ticket, just a human traveling companion, and both of you must travel during off-peak hours.

PET CAB
212-491-5300

Run by a former dog trainer, this pet-friendly service can handle any canine transportation need, whether it's a Jaguar to whiz you and your saluki to the Fisher's Island ferry or a stretcher-equipped van for getting you both to the vet. The company's connection with a (people's) limo service allows it to offer a wide variety of services, and they are glad to help the elderly. These people are friends indeed: They can go with you if you have to have your animal put to sleep and will provide referrals for grief therapy. *Cost:* from $23.

WORLD WIDE PET TRANSPORT
718-539-5543

This company provides door-to-door pickup and delivery for local and long-distance destinations. Airport arrangements (including international shipping) are available, as well as surface transport for pets who prefer not to fly. *Cost:* $60 an hour. A Manhattan-Hamptons run is around $275.

Vacation Guides

If you want to take a vacation with Rex, it helps to know ahead of time what hotels and motels accept pets. Consult the following guides, available through mail order or at pet supply shops and bookstores:

HAVE DOG, WILL TRAVEL
DogGone
P.O. Box 651159
Vero Beach, FL 32965

A newsletter on travel destinations and free activities for you and your dog. *Cost:* $24 for a year's subscription of six issues.

ON THE ROAD AGAIN WITH MAN'S BEST FRIENDS: NEW ENGLAND
by Dawn and Robert Habgood
Dawbert Press
Box 2758
Duxbury, MA 12331

Inns, hotels, resorts, and motels where you and Rover are welcome.

PETS ALLOWED
MFC
9 Greenmeadow Drive #FD
N. Billerica, MA 01862

This guide lists hotels and motels all over the country that welcome dogs. *Cost:* $10.

TAKE YOUR PET USA
Art Co. Publishing
12 Channel Street
Boston, MA 02210

A national guide to dog-friendly accommodations.

TOURING WITH TOWSER
Quaker Professional Service
TWT, Department PGP
585 Hawthorne Court
Galesburg, IL 614011

Cost: $3.00

Travel agents

If you don't know where you want to go, there are travel agents that specialize in dog-oriented trips. One is:

FRESH POND TRAVEL
344 Boston Post Road
Marlboro, MA 01752
800-225-4897

This travel agent can arrange three days on Martha's Vineyard for around $69 per person, double occupancy.

Care to fly to Mexico City for the dog show? Round-trip airfare for you both, with five nights' accommodations, is only $819. Traveling solo? Deduct $100.

Camps

The places listed below offer fun and training for you and Binky:

BAUMAN'S CANINE CAMP
296 Lake Wallkill Road
Sussex, NJ 07461
201-702-1149

Usually held in mid-May at the Kutz Camp Institute in Warwick, New York, this camp provides a week of training for you and your dog. In addition to dog instruction at all levels, horseback riding is available to owners. *Cost:* from $645 including lodging and all meals for you and your dog. For movie junkies with cabin fever, there's a drive-in five minutes away.

CAMP GONE TO THE DOGS
Honey Loring
RR 1, Box 958
Putney, VT 05346
802-387-5673

The early June program can include lectures on home-opathy, natural flea control, and dog CPR. *Cost:* approximately $600 per person and dog.

WIZ KID DOG CAMP
4 Brookside Place
Westport CT 06880
203-226-9556

Usually five days in October at a children's camp in
Pennsylvania. *Cost:* From $535 per person and dog for
program and dog lodging; owner lodging is extra.

When the Dog Dies

Sadly, there comes a time when your dog dies. It might be the result of an accident, illness, or your own decision to put the animal to sleep. At times like these, a good, sensitive veterinarian is invaluable. Although there is no way to make the loss of a pet easy, services are available to help you through the ordeal.

Counseling

ASPCA
424 East 92nd Street
212-876-7700

Grief counselor Paula Anreder can help you during this difficult time.

BIDE-A-WEE
410 East 38th Street
212-532-6395

Call for an appointment with their bereavement counseling service.

PETS
Box 9303
Longview, TX 75608

Write them to order *Please Ease the Sorrow,* a book to help you through the loss. The book costs $20.

VANCOUVER DOG TRAINING SCHOOL
120 Riverside Drive
212-877-7116

Owner Pat McGregor works with a social worker and will help you get over the loss of your pet.

Cemeteries and Crematories

ABBEY GLEN PET MEMORIAL PARK
Route 2, Box 512
Lafayette, NJ 07848
800-972-3118

In a beautiful, picturesque setting, this establishment offers a full line of caskets and urns, a viewing room, individual burials and cremations, and transportation.

ALDSTATE PET CREMATION SERVICES
306 83rd Street
Brooklyn
718-748-2104

Aldstate will pick up for cremation in all boroughs and return the ashes to you four days later in your choice of urn: standard metal floral, wood, bronze, or pewter. *Cost:* from $130.

BIDE-A-WEE PET MEMORIAL PARK
118 Old Country Road
Westhampton, NY 11977
516-325-0219

3300 Beltagh Avenue
Wantagh, NY
516-785-6153

Both places are nonprofit burial parks run by the Bide-a-Wee folks. You can have your dog buried in a private plot or cremated here. This sympathetic organization, whose motto is "Where your love endures," also offers bereavement counseling. *Cost:* from $125, including pickup.

When the Dog Dies

HARTSDALE CANINE CEMETERY
75 North Central Avenue
Hartsdale, NY 10530
914-949-2583

Established in 1896, this is the oldest pet cemetery in
the United States. They will arrange for pickup. Their
traditional funeral includes a viewing and service.

REGENCY FOREST PET MEMORIAL
760 Middle Country Road
Middle Island, NY 11953
800-372-PETS

A full-service cemetery and crematorium that allows
you to visit your burial plot at any time. *Cost:* from
$500 for pickup, plot, casket, and burial; from $170 for
individual cremation and urn.

Good Reading

There's nothing more satisfying than sitting and reading with a canine companion curled at your feet. While you're at it, you can read about dogs, too:

Magazines

DOG
4977 Midway Lane
Marshall, WI 53559

DOG FANCY
2401 Beverly Boulevard
Los Angeles, CA 90057

"Dog Care for the Responsible Owner"

DOG WORLD
300 West Adams Street
Chicago, IL 60606

Training tips, health information, breeder information

GOOD DOG
P.O. Box 31292
Charleston, SC 29417

NATURAL PET, ALTERNATIVE CARE
P.O. Box 531
Trilby, FL 33593

PURE-BRED DOGS, THE AMERICAN KENNEL GAZETTE
51 Madison Avenue
New York, NY 10010

PETHOUSE
215 Lexington Avenue
13th Floor
New York, NY 10016

Devoted exclusively to New York City pet owners

Books

Below is a list of books about dogs. (For books specifically about training, see page 28, and for vacation guides, see pages 88-89).

American Kennel Club, *The Complete Dog Book* (Howell Book House)

Bulanda, Susan, *Everything You Always Wanted to Know About Dogs: Canine Source Book* (Doral Publishers)

Carras, Roger, *The Roger Carras Dog Book* (M. Evans and Company)

Evans, Mark, *The ASPCA Pet Care Guide for Kids* (Dorling Kindersley)

Grossman, Lloyd, *The Dog's Tale: A History of Man's Best Friend* (BBC Books)

Hearne, Vicki, *Bandit: Dossier of a Dangerous Dog* (HarperCollins)

Knight, Eric, *Lassie Come Home* (Henry Holt)

Kovary, Robin, *Good Puppy: How to Raise, Train, and Protect the Puppy You Love* (Direct Book Service)

McCaig, Donald, *Nop's Hope* (Crown Publishers)

Good Reading

McCall, Bruce, *Sit: The Dog Portraits of Thierry Poncelet* (Western Publishers)

McGinnis, Terri, *The Well Dog Book* (Random House)

Poortvliet, Rien, *Dogs* (Harry N. Abrams)

Reynolds, R., *Dog Bites! Canine Cuisine* (Berkley Books)

Rogerson, John, *Training Your Best Friend* (Howell Book House)

Thomas, Elizabeth Marshall, *The Hidden Life of Dogs* (Houghton Mifflin)

And Good Watching

The Pet Department: Mon to Fri.: 2:30 P.M. to 3:00 P.M.

This FX Cable Television series is co-hosted by Steve Walker and Jack the Dog. The program features a field reporter, "Animal Road Tests" (2- to 3-minute special pieces on various animals), and a weekly question and answer session with visiting vets.

Useful Sources

Following are some of the dog-oriented organizations in and out of the city that you might find useful:

AMERICAN KENNEL CLUB
51 Madison Avenue
212-696-8200

This is a source for information on breeds, breeders, dog shows, and the Canine Good Citizen Programs.

ASPCA
424 East 92nd Street
212-876-7700

Services include adoptions, training, a veterinary clinic, spaying and neutering, pet-assisted therapy, shelters, bereavement counseling, and much more.

BIDE-A-WEE
410 East 38th Street
212-532-4455

A source for shelters, veterinary clinics, spaying and neutering, training, adoptions, memorial parks, pet-assisted therapy, bereavement counseling, and more.

FRIENDS OF ANIMALS
800-321-PETS

They will give you names of veterinarians near you who will neuter or spay your dog at reduced rates.

HUMANE SOCIETY OF NEW YORK
306 East 59th Street
212-752-4840

Another source for adoptions, clinics, spaying and neutering, and animal-rights education.

PETA
(People for the Ethical Treatment of Animals)
P.O. Box 42516
Washington, D.C. 20015
310-770-PETA

An activist group that works for animal rights.

POWARS (Pet Owners with Aids Resource Services)
P.O. Box 1116
Madison Square Station, NY 10159
212-744-0842

This organization is dedicated to helping people with AIDS take care of their pets: Volunteers will feed and walk the dog and take it to the vet.

Phone Numbers

AMERICAN DOG TRAINER NETWORK HELPLINE
212-727-7257

They offer free referrals for trainers, pet-care services, behavioral tips, rescue-club listings, and spaying and neutering information.

ANIMAL MEDICAL CENTER
212-838-8100

A twenty-four-hour emergency medical service.

ASPCA
212-722-3620

Locates lost dogs.

NYC EMERGENCY PICK-UP
718-649-8600

Call if you've found or rescued a dog.

POISON CONTROL CENTER
800-548-2423

A twenty-four-hour poison helpline.

Afterword

By now you should have a very good idea of what the city has to offer you and your dog. The most important thing to understand is that it is your responsibility to be an informed dog owner. Your dog can't go out and shop for its own food or clothes, and it cannot sit down and explain which veterinarian it prefers, even with the help of the animal psychics and communicators.

We hope you use the information in this book as a first step toward discovering great dog places, services, and people. Owning a dog in New York City can be rewarding. It helps keep the city in scale, and it is a wonderful way to get out and meet people—to make the city feel more manageable and less intimidating. So pick up the leash and take Fifi for a walk. Enjoy the city and your city dog.

ALSO AVAILABLE FROM CITY & COMPANY

How to Make New York a Better Place to Live
A Handbook for Resident Angels

Good & Cheap Ethnic Eats Under $10
In and Around New York

How to Meet a Mensch in New York

C I T Y   &   C O M P A N Y
N E W   Y O R K